Ocean Breeze Sleeveless Sweater for Mother

Skill Level

EASY

Sizes

Woman's extra-small (small, medium, large, extra-large, 2X-large, 3X-large, 4X-large) Instructions are given for smallest size, with larger sizes in parentheses. When only 1 number is given, it applies to all sizes.

Finished Measurement

Chest: 32 (36, 40, 44, 48, 52, 56, 60) inches

Materials

- TLC Cotton Plus medium weight yarn (3.5 oz/178 yds/100g per skein): 3 (4, 5, 5, 5, 6, 7, 7) skeins navy #3859
- Size 5 (3.75mm) straight and 16-inch circular needles
- Size 7 (4.5mm) needles or size needed to obtain gauge
- Stitch holders

MEDIUM

Gauge

20 sts and 28 rows = 4 inches/10cm in St st on larger needles
To save time, take time to check gauge.

Special Abbreviations

Mirrored dec (mirrored decrease):

K1, k2tog, knit to last 3 sts, sl 1, k1, psso, k1.

M1 (Make 1):

Inc 1 st by picking up horizontal strand between last st worked and next st, k1-tbl. **Note:** *Work all inc 1 st in from the edge.*

Pattern Stitches

1 x 1 Rib (in rows on odd number of sts)
Row 1 (RS): K1, *p1, k1; rep from * across.
Row 2: P1, * k1, p1; rep from * across.
Rep Rows 1 and 2 for pat.

1 x 1 Rib (in rnds on even number of sts)
Rnd 1: *K1, p1; rep from * around.
Rep Rnd 1 for pat.

Back

With smaller needles, cast on 79 (89, 99, 109, 119, 129, 139, 149) sts. Work 1 x 1 Rib for 1½ inches, ending by working a WS row.

Change to larger needles.

Work in St st for ½ inch.

Dec 1 st at each edge on next row then [every 6th row] 3 times. (71, 81, 91, 101, 111, 121, 131, 141 sts)

Work even for 4 (4, 5, 5, 6, 6, 7, 7) inches.

Inc by M1 at each edge on next row then [every 6th row] 3 times. (79, 89, 99, 109, 119, 129, 139, 149 sts)

Work even until back measures 14 (14½, 15, 15½, 16, 16, 17, 17) inches from cast-on edge.

Shape armhole

Bind off 4 (5, 6, 7, 9, 11, 11, 12) sts at beg of next 2 rows.

Work mirrored dec [every RS row] 3 (5, 7, 8, 9, 11, 11, 12) times. (65, 69, 73, 79, 83, 85, 95, 101 sts)

Work even until armhole measures 7 (7½, 8, 8½, 9, 9½, 10, 10½) inches, ending by working a WS row.

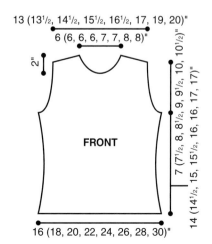

13 (13½, 14½, 15½, 16½, 17, 19, 20)"
6 (6, 6, 6, 7, 7, 8, 8)"
2"
FRONT
7 (7½, 8, 8½, 9, 9½, 10, 10½)"
14 (14½, 15, 15½, 16, 16, 17, 17)"
16 (18, 20, 22, 24, 26, 28, 30)"

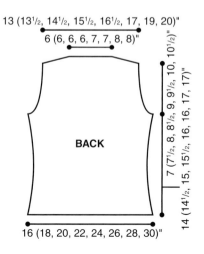

13 (13½, 14½, 15½, 16½, 17, 19, 20)"
6 (6, 6, 6, 7, 7, 8, 8)"
BACK
7 (7½, 8, 8½, 9, 9½, 10, 10½)"
14 (14½, 15, 15½, 16, 16, 17, 17)"
16 (18, 20, 22, 24, 26, 28, 30)"

Shape shoulder

Row 1 (RS): Knit to last 6 (6, 7, 8, 8, 8, 9, 10) sts, turn.

Row 2: Purl to last 6 (6, 7, 8, 8, 8, 9, 10) sts, turn.

Row 3: Knit to last 12 (12, 14, 16, 16, 16, 18, 20) sts, turn.

Row 4: Purl to last 12 (12, 14, 16, 16, 16, 18, 20) sts, turn.

Row 5: Knit to last 17 (19, 21, 24, 24, 25, 27, 30) sts, turn.

Row 6: Purl to last 17 (19, 21, 24, 24, 25, 27, 30) sts.

Place center 31 (31, 31, 31, 35, 35, 41, 41) sts on holder for back neck.

Place 17 (19, 21, 24, 24, 25, 27, 30) sts on each side on holders for shoulders.

Front

Work same as back until armhole measures 5 (5½, 6, 6½, 7, 7½, 8, 8½) inches, ending by working a WS row.

Shape neck

Knit 22 (24, 26, 29, 29, 30, 32, 35) sts, join 2nd ball of yarn, knit center 21 (21, 21, 21, 25, 25, 31, 31) sts and place them on a holder, knit rem 22 (24, 26, 29, 29, 30, 32, 35) sts. Working on both sides at once with separate balls of yarn, dec 1 st at neck edge [every RS row] 5 times. Work even until front measures same as back to shoulder shaping, ending by working a WS row.

Shape shoulder

Row 1 (RS): Knit across first shoulder; on 2nd shoulder, knit to last 6 (6, 7, 8, 8, 8, 9, 10) sts, turn.

Row 2: Purl across first shoulder; on 2nd shoulder, purl to last 6 (6, 7, 8, 8, 8, 9, 10) sts, turn.

Row 3: Knit across first shoulder; on 2nd shoulder, knit to last 12 (12, 14, 16, 16, 16, 18, 20) sts, turn.

Row 4: Purl across first shoulder; on 2nd shoulder, purl to last 12 (12, 14, 16, 16, 16, 18, 20) sts, turn.

Row 5: Knit across first shoulder; on 2nd shoulder, place 17 (19, 21, 24, 24, 25, 27, 30) sts on holder, turn.

Row 6: Place rem 17 (19, 21, 24, 24, 25, 27, 30) sts on holder.

Assembly

Join shoulders using 3-needle bind-off (see page 31).

Sew side seams.

Edgings

Neck edging

Hold with RS and right shoulder seam facing you, with circular needle, knit across 31 (31, 31, 31, 35, 35, 41, 41) sts on holder for back, pick up and knit 16 sts along side of neck; knit across center 21 (21, 21, 21, 25, 25, 31, 31) sts on holder for front, pick up and knit 16 sts along side of neck. (84, 84, 84, 84, 92, 92, 104, 104 sts)

Join and work 1 x 1 Rib in rnds until ribbing measures 3 inches or desired length. **_Note:_** _Rib will stretch and become shorter when worn._

Bind off loosely in pat.

Armhole Edging

Hold with RS and underarm seam facing, with circular needle join at underarm. Pick up and knit 39 (42, 46, 49, 54, 58, 61, 69) sts from underarm to shoulder; then pick up and knit 39 (42, 46, 49, 54, 58, 61, 69) sts from the shoulder to the underarm. (78, 84, 92, 98, 108, 116, 122, 138 sts)

Join and work 1 x 1 Rib in rnds until ribbing measures 1 inch.

Bind off loosely in pat. ■

Ocean Breeze Sleeveless Sweater for Girls

Skill Level

EASY

Sizes

Girl's 4 (6, 8/10, 12/14) Instructions are given for smallest size, with larger sizes in parentheses. When only 1 number is given, it applies to all sizes.

Finished Measurement

Chest: 26 (28, 30, 32) inches

Materials

- TLC Cotton Plus medium weight yarn (3.5 oz/178 yds/100g per skein): 2 (2, 2, 3) skeins medium blue #3811
- Size 5 (3.75mm) straight and 16-inch circular needles
- Size 7 (4.5mm) needles or size needed to obtain gauge
- Stitch holders

Gauge

20 sts and 28 rows = 4 inches/10cm in St st on larger needles
To save time, take time to check gauge.

Special Abbreviation

Mirrored dec (mirrored decrease):

K1, k2tog, knit to last 3 sts, sl 1, k1, psso, k1.

Note: *Work all dec 1 st in from the edge.*

Pattern Stitches

1 x 1 Rib (in rows on odd number of sts)

Row 1 (RS): K1, *p1, k1; rep from * across.

Row 2: P1, * k1, p1; rep from * across.

Rep Rows 1 and 2 for pat.

1 x 1 Rib (in rnds on even number of sts)

Rnd 1: *K1, p1; rep from * around.

Rep Rnd 1 for pat.

Back

With smaller needles, cast on 59 (63, 67, 71) sts. Work 1 x 1 Rib for 2 inches, ending by working a WS row.

Change to larger needles.

Next row (RS): Knit inc 6 (8, 8, 8) sts evenly across. (65, 71, 75, 79 sts)

Work in St st until back measures 9 (10½, 12, 14) inches from cast-on edge.

Shape armholes

Bind off 4 (4, 4, 4) sts at beg of next 2 rows.

Work mirrored dec [every RS row] 3 (3, 3, 3) times. (51, 57, 61, 65 sts)

Work even until armhole measures 5½ (6, 6½, 7) inches, ending by working a RS row.

Purl across 12 (15, 17, 19) sts and place on holder for shoulder; purl center 27 and place on holder for back neck; purl rem 12 (15, 17, 19) and place sts on holder for other shoulder.

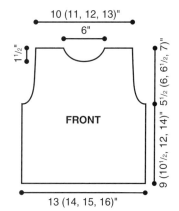

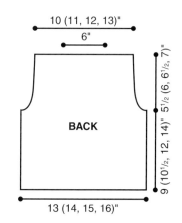

Front

Work same as back until armhole measures 4 (4½, 5, 5½) inches, ending after a WS row.

Shape neck

Knit 18 (21, 23, 25) sts, join 2nd ball of yarn, knit center 15 sts and place them onto a holder, knit rem 18 (21, 23, 25) sts. Work both sides at once with separate balls of yarn. At each neck edge, [bind off 2 sts] 3 times. (12, 15, 17, 19 sts)

Work even until front measures same as back to shoulders.

Assembly

Join shoulders using 3-needle bind-off (see page 31).

Sew side seams.

Edgings

Neck edging

Hold with RS and right shoulder seam facing you, with circular needle, knit across 27 sts on holder for back neck, pick up and knit 13 sts along side of neck; knit across center 15 sts, pick up and knit 13 sts along side of neck. (68 sts)

Join and work 1 x 1 Rib in rnds until ribbing measures 2 inches or desired length. Bind off loosely in pat.

Armhole edging

Hold with RS and underarm seam facing, with circular needle, join yarn at underarm. Pick up and knit 31 (35, 37, 39) sts from underarm to shoulder; then pick up and knit 31 (35, 37, 39) sts from the shoulder to the underarm. (62, 70, 74, 78 sts)

Join and work 1 x 1 Rib in rnds until ribbing measures 1 inch or desired length.

Bind off loosely in pat. ∎

Ocean Breeze Sleeveless Sweater for Baby

Skill Level

EASY

Sizes

Baby's/toddler's 6 months (1 year, 2 years) Instructions are given for smallest size, with larger sizes in parentheses. When only 1 number is given, it applies to all sizes.

Finished Measurement

Chest: 20 (22, 24) inches

Materials

- TLC Cotton Plus medium weight yarn (3.5 oz/186 yds/100g per skein): 2 (2, 2) skeins light blue #3810
- Size 5 (3.75mm) needles
- Size 7 (4.5mm) needles or size needed to obtain gauge
- 4 (6, 6) ½-inch Camp Grandma gingham heart buttons #24057 from JHB International

Gauge

20 sts/ and 28 rows = 4 inches/10cm in St st on larger needles
To save time, take time to check gauge.

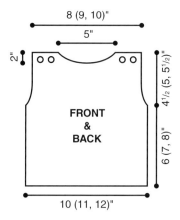

Special Abbreviation

Mirrored dec (mirrored decrease):
K1, k2tog, knit to last 3 sts, sl 1, k 1, psso, k1.

Pattern Stitch

1 x 1 Rib (in rows on odd number of sts)
Row 1 (RS): K1, *p1, k1; rep from * across.
Row 2: P1, * k1, p1; rep from * across.
Rep Rows 1 and 2 for pat.

Back

With smaller needles, cast on 51 (55, 61) sts. Work 1 x 1 Rib for 1 inch, ending by working a WS row.

Change to larger needles.

Work in St st until back measures 6 (7, 8) inches from cast-on edge.

Shape armhole

Bind off 2 sts at beg of next 2 rows.

Work mirrored dec [every RS row] 3 (3, 3) times. (41, 45, 51 sts)

Work even until armhole measures 2½ (3, 3½) inches.

Shape neck

Knit 15 (17, 20) sts, join 2nd ball of yarn; knit center 11 sts and place them on a holder; knit rem 15 (17, 20) sts. Working both sides at once with separate balls of yarn, dec 1 st at neck edge [every RS row] 7 times. (8, 10, 13 sts)

For back shoulder tab: Knit every row for 6 rows (3 ridges).
Bind off.

Front

Work same as back to shoulder tab.

For front shoulder tab: Knit every row for 4 rows (2 ridges).

Next row (buttonhole): K6 (4, 6), yo, k2tog, k0 (4, 5) for first shoulder; k0 (4, 5), k2tog, yo, k6 (4, 6).
Knit across both shoulders.
Bind off.

Edgings

Back neck edging

With RS of back facing, pick up and knit 14 sts along right back neck edge, knit center 11 sts from holder, pick up and knit 14 sts along left back neck edge. (39 sts)

Work 1 x 1 Rib for 5 rows.

Bind off in pat.

Front neck edging

Hold with RS of front facing, pick up and knit 14 sts along left-front neck edge, knit center 11 sts from holder, pick up and knit 14 sts along right-front neck edge. (39 sts)

Next row: P1, *k1, p1; rep from * across.

Next row (buttonhole row): K1, p1, yo, k2tog, work ribbing to last 4 sts, yo, k2tog, p1, k1.

Beg with Row 2, work 3 rows of 1 x 1 Rib.

Bind off in pat.

Assembly

Sew buttons to back shoulder tabs to correspond to buttonholes. Button shoulders in place so that tabs are now overlapped.

Armhole edging

Hold with RS facing, beg at underarm, pick up and knit 49 (55, 59) sts around armhole opening, picking up through both layers at shoulder tabs and ending at underarm.

Work 5 rows 1 x 1 Rib.

Bind off in pat.

Finishing

Sew side seams. ■

Lacy Stripe Cardigan for Mother

Skill Level

INTERMEDIATE

Sizes

Woman's small (medium, large, extra-large, 2X-large, 3X-large, 4X-large) Instructions are given for the smallest size, with larger sizes in parentheses. When only 1 number is given, it applies to all sizes.

Finished Measurement

Chest: 36 (40, 44, 48, 52, 56, 60) inches

Materials

- TLC Cotton Plus medium weight yarn (3.5 oz/178 yds/100g per skein): 2 (3, 3, 3, 4, 4, 4) skeins each red #3907 (A), kiwi #3643 (B), tangerine #3252 (C), tan #3303 (D)
- Size 7 (4.5mm) 29-inch circular needle or size needed to obtain gauge
- Stitch markers
- Stitch holders
- 24 inches 1-inch-wide organza ribbon
- Sewing needle and matching thread

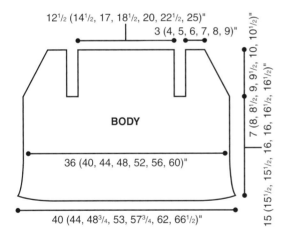

12¹/₂ (14¹/₂, 17, 18¹/₂, 20, 22¹/₂, 25)"

3 (4, 5, 6, 7, 8, 9)"

7 (8, 8¹/₂, 9, 9¹/₂, 10, 10¹/₂)"

BODY

36 (40, 44, 48, 52, 56, 60)"

15 (15¹/₂, 15¹/₂, 16, 16, 16¹/₂, 16¹/₂)"

40 (44, 48³/₄, 53, 57³/₄, 62, 66¹/₂)"

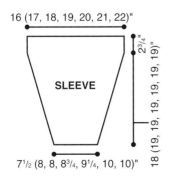

16 (17, 18, 19, 20, 21, 22)"

2³/₄"

SLEEVE

18 (19, 19, 19, 19, 19, 19)"

7¹/₂ (8, 8, 8³/₄, 9¹/₄, 10, 10)"

Gauge

18 sts = 4 inches/10cm in Lace pat
To save time, take time to check gauge.

Pattern Stitches

Lace

Row 1 (RS): Join new color, knit.

Rows 2 and 3: Knit.

Row 4: Purl.

Row 5: K1, *yo, k2tog; rep from * to last st, k1.

Row 6: Purl.

Rep Rows 1–6 for pat.

Stripe Sequence

Work in Lace pat in following color sequence:

*6 rows A,

6 rows B,

6 rows C,

6 rows D.

Rep from * for stripe sequence.

Pattern Notes

Work dec at neck edge 4 sts in from front edge, keeping 4 edge sts in garter st.

Body of sweater is worked in 1 piece to underarms, then divided and shaped for armholes and neck.

Front edging is included in the body sts.

Sleeves are knit flat then sewn to body.

Body

With A, cast on 180 (200, 220, 240, 260, 280, 300) sts.

Next row: K4, place marker, work in Lace pat to last 4 sts, place marker, k4.

Keeping first and last 4 sts in garter st and sts between markers in Lace pat, continue in pat as established working Stripe Sequence until piece measures 7 inches from cast-on edge, ending by working a Row 2 or 6.

Shape waist

Next row: K4 sts, work in Lace pat to marker; dec 18 (20, 22, 24, 26, 28, 30) sts evenly spaced, k4. (162, 180, 198, 216, 234, 252, 270 sts)

Continue even in pats as established until body measures 15 (15½, 15½, 16, 16, 16½, 16½) inches, ending by working a Row 2 or 6.

Divide for armholes

Work in pat across 29 (33, 37, 42, 47, 51, 55) sts for right front and place sts on holder; bind off next 24 sts for underarm; work in pat across 56 (66, 76, 84, 92, 102, 112) sts for back; bind off next 24 sts for underarm; work in pat across rem 29 (33, 37, 42, 47, 51, 55) sts for right front and place sts on holder. Cut yarn.

Back

Work in pat as established on back sts until armhole measures 6½ (7½, 8, 8½, 9, 9½, 10) inches, ending with a Row 2 or 6.

Back neck shaping

Next row: Work in pat across 13 (18, 23, 27, 31, 36, 41) sts, place marker, knit center 30 sts, work in pat across 13 (18, 23, 27, 31, 36, 41) sts.

Rep last row until armhole measures 7 (8, 8½, 9, 9½, 10, 10½) inches.

Bind off all sts.

Right Front

Place right front sts on needle.

Neck shaping

Note: Work dec at neck edge 4 sts in from edge, keeping 4 sts at center front in garter st.

Continue in pat as established, dec 1 st at neck edge [every 4th row] 8 (8, 8, 8, 15, 15, 15) times, then [every RS row] 5 (7, 7, 7, 0, 0, 0) times. (13, 18, 23, 27, 31, 36, 41 sts)

Work even until front measures same as back to shoulders.

Bind off all sts.

Left Front

Place left front sts on needle.

Neck shaping

Note: Work dec at neck edge 4 sts in from edge, keeping 4 sts at center front in garter st.

Continue in pat as established, dec 1 st at neck edge [every 4th row] 8 (8, 8, 8, 15, 15, 15) times, then [every RS row] 5 (7, 7, 7, 0, 0, 0) times. (13, 18, 23, 27, 31, 36, 41 sts)

Work even until front measures same as back to shoulders.

Bind off all sts.

Sleeves

With A cast on 34 (36, 36, 40, 42, 46, 46) sts. Knit 2 rows.

Work in Lace pat and *at the same time* inc 1 st at each edge [every 4th row] 19 (20, 23, 23, 24, 24, 27) times. (72, 76, 82, 86, 90, 94, 100 sts)

Work even until sleeve measures 18 (19, 19, 19, 19, 19, 19) inches.

Place marker at each edge to mark underarm placement.

Work even for 2¾ inches.

Bind off all sts.

Finishing

Sew shoulder seams.

Sew sleeve seam from cuff to markers.

Sew sleeve into armhole, matching center of top of sleeve to shoulder seam and placing markers at center of armhole on body.

Cut ribbon in half. Sew 1 piece to inside of each front edge below first neck dec. ∎

Lacy Stripe Cardigan for Girls

Skill Level

INTERMEDIATE

Sizes

Girl's 4 (6, 8/10, 12/14) Instructions are given for the smallest size, with larger sizes in parentheses. When only 1 number is given, it applies to all sizes.

Finished Measurement

Chest: 26 (28, 30, 32) inches

Materials

- TLC Cotton Plus medium weight yarn (3.5 oz/178 yds/100g per skein): 1 (1, 1, 2) skein(s) each spruce #3503 (A), lavender #3590 (B), medium blue #3811 (C), kiwi #3643 (D)
- Size 7 (4.5mm) 29-inch circular needle or size needed to obtain gauge
- Stitch holders
- 20 inches 1-inch-wide organza ribbon
- Sewing needle and matching thread

Gauge

18 sts = 4 inches/10cm in Lace pat
To save time, take time to check gauge.

Pattern Stitches

Lace

Row 1 (RS): Join new color, knit.

Rows 2 and 3: Knit.

Row 4: Purl.

Row 5: K1, *yo, k2tog; rep from * to last st, k1.

Row 6: Purl.

Rep Rows 1–6 for pat.

Stripe Sequence

Work Lace pat in following color sequence:

*6 rows A,

6 rows B,

6 rows C,

6 rows D.

Rep from * for stripe sequence.

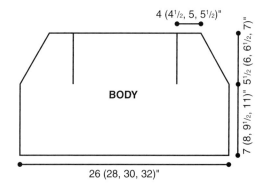

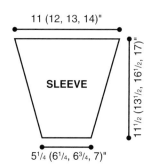

Pattern Notes

Work dec at neck edge 4 sts in from front edge, keeping 4 edge sts in garter st.

Body of sweater is worked in 1 piece to underarms, then divided and shaped for armholes and neck.

Front edging is included in the body sts. Sleeves are knit flat then sewn to body.

Body

With A, cast on 118 (126, 136, 144) sts.

Next row: K4, place marker, work in Lace pat to last 4 sts, place marker, k4.

Keeping first and last 4 sts in garter st, and sts between markers in Lace pat, continue in pat as established working Stripe Sequence until piece measures approximately 7 (8, 9½, 11) inches from cast-on edge, ending by working a Row 2 or 6.

Divide for armholes

Work in pat across 29 (32, 34, 36) sts for right front and place on holder; work in pat across next 60 (62, 68, 72) sts for back. Place rem 29 (32, 34, 36) sts on holder for left front.

Back

Work in pat as established on back sts until armhole measures 5 (5½, 6, 6½) inches, ending by working a Row 2 or 6.

Back neck edging

Next row: Work in pat across 19 (20, 23, 25) sts, place marker, knit center 22 sts, work in pattern across 19 (20, 23, 25) sts.

Rep last row until armhole measures 5½ (6, 6½, 7) inches.

Bind off all sts.

Right Front

Place right front sts on needles.

Neck shaping

Note: *Work dec at neck edge 4 sts in from edge, keeping 4 sts at center front in garter st.*

Continue in pat as established, dec 1 st on next RS row, then [every 4th row] 5 times and [every RS row] 5 (6, 6, 6) times. (19, 20, 23, 25 sts)

Work even until front measures same as back to shoulder.

Bind off all sts.

Left Front

Place left front sts on needles.

Neck shaping

Note: *Work dec at neck edge 4 sts in from edge, keeping 4 sts at center front in garter st.*

Continue in pat as established, dec 1 st at neck edge on next RS row, then [every 4th row] 5 times and [every RS row] 5 (6, 6, 6, 6) times. (19, 20, 23, 25 sts)

Work even until front measure same as back to shoulder.

Bind off all sts.

Sleeve

With A cast on 24 (28, 30, 32) sts. Work in Lace pat and *at the same time* inc 1 st at each edge [every 4th row] 13 (13, 14, 16) times. (50, 54, 58, 64 sts)

Work even until sleeve measures 11½ (13½, 16½, 17) inches.

Bind off all sts.

Finishing

Sew shoulder seams.

Sew sleeve in armhole, matching center top of sleeve to shoulder seam.

Cut ribbon in half. Sew 1 piece to inside of each front edge just below first neck dec. ■

Lacy Stripe Cardigan for Baby

Skill Level

INTERMEDIATE

Sizes

Baby's/toddler's 6 months (1 year, 2 years) Instructions are given for the smallest size, with larger sizes in parentheses. When only 1 number is given, it applies to all sizes.

Finished Measurement

Chest: 20 (22, 24) inches

Materials

- TLC Cotton Plus medium weight yarn (3.5 oz/178 yds/100g per skein): 1 skein each light blue #3810 (A), lavender #3590 (B), medium rose #3707 (C), light rose #3706 (D)
- Size 7 (4.5mm) 29-inch circular needle or size needed to obtain gauge
- Stitch holders
- 20 inches 1-inch-wide organza ribbon
- Sewing needle and matching thread

Gauge

18 sts = 4 inches/10cm in Lace pat
To save time, take time to check gauge.

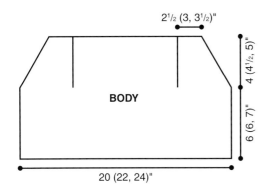

2½ (3, 3½)"

4 (4½, 5)"

6 (6, 7)"

BODY

20 (22, 24)"

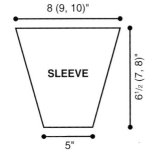

8 (9, 10)"

6½ (7, 8)"

SLEEVE

5"

Pattern Stitches

Lace

Row 1 (RS): Join new color, knit.

Rows 2 and 3: Knit.

Row 4: Purl.

Row 5: K1, *yo, k2tog; rep from * to last st, k1.

Row 6: Purl.

Rep Rows 1–6 for pat.

Stripe Sequence

Work Lace pat in following color sequence:

*6 rows A,

6 rows B,

6 rows C,

6 rows D.

Rep from * for stripe sequence.

Pattern Notes

Work dec at neck edge 4 sts in from front edge, keeping 4 edge sts in garter st.

Body of sweater is worked in 1 piece to underarms, then divided and shaped for armholes and neck.

Front edging is included in the body sts. Sleeves are knit flat then sewn to body.

Body

With A, cast on 90 (100, 108) sts.

Next row: K4, place marker, work in Lace pat to last 4 sts, place marker, k4.

Keeping first and last 4 sts in garter st and sts between markers in Lace pat, continue in pat as established working Stripe Sequence until piece measures approximately 6 (6, 7) inches from cast-on edge, ending by working Row 2 or 6.

Divide for armholes

Work in pat across 23 (25, 27) sts for right front and place sts on holder; work in pat across next 44 (50, 54) sts for back. Place rem 23 (25, 27) sts on holder for left front.

Back

Work in pat as established on back sts until armhole measures 3½ (4, 4½) inches, ending with a Row 2 or 6.

Neck edging

Next row: Work in pat across 11 (14, 16) sts, place marker, knit center 22 sts, work in pat across 11 (14, 16) sts.

Rep last row until armhole measures 4 (4½, 5) inches.

Bind off all sts.

Right Front

Place right front sts on needles.

Neck shaping

Note: *Work dec at neck edge 4 sts in from edge, keeping 4 sts at center front in garter st.*

Continue in pat as established, dec 1 st at neck edge [every RS row] 11 times. (11, 14, 16 sts)

Work even until front measures same as back to shoulders.

Bind off all sts.

Left Front

Place left front sts on needles.

Neck shaping

Note: *Work dec at neck edge 4 sts in from edge, keeping 4 sts at center front in garter st.*

Continue in pat as established, dec 1 st at neck edge [every RS row] 11 times. (11, 14, 16 sts) Work even until front measures same as back to shoulders.

Bind off all sts.

Sleeves

With A cast on 22 sts.

Work in Lace pat and *at the same time* inc 1 st at each edge [every 4th row] 7 (9, 12) times. (36, 40, 46 sts)

Work even until sleeve measures 6½ (7, 8) inches.

Bind off all sts.

Finishing

Sew shoulder seams.

Sew sleeve into armhole, matching center of top of sleeve to shoulder seam.

Cut ribbon in half. Sew 1 piece to inside of each front edge just below first neck dec. ■

Skill Level

EASY

Sizes

Woman's small (medium, large, extra-large, 2X-large, 3X-large, 4X-large) Instructions are given for smallest size, with larger sizes in parentheses. When only 1 number is given, it applies to all sizes.

Finished Measurement

Chest: 36 (40, 44, 48, 52, 56, 60) inches

Materials

- Lion Brand Microspun lightweight yarn (2.5 oz/168 yds/70g per skein): 5 (6, 7, 8, 9, 10, 10) skeins turquoise #148
- Size 5 (3.75mm) circular or straight needles or size needed to obtain gauge
- Size E/4 (3.5mm) crochet hook (for button loop)
- Stitch holders
- ¾-inch flat button
- 5 (5mm) beads (for flower trim)
- Sewing needle and matching thread

Gauge

22 sts and 32 rows = 4 inches/10cm in Double Moss pat
To save time, take time to check gauge.

Pattern Stitch

Double Moss (multiple of 4 sts + 2)
Row 1: K1, * k2, p2; rep from * across, end k1.
Row 2: P1, * k2, p2; rep from * across, end p1.
Row 3: K1, *p2, k2; rep from * across, end k1.
Row 4: P1, *p2, k2; rep from * across, end p1.
Rep Rows 1–4 for pat.

Pattern Notes

Sweater is worked from lower front hem edges to lower back hem edge with sts cast on at outer edges for the sleeves.
When piece is completed, side and underarm seams are sewn.

Left Front

Cast on 50 (54, 60, 66, 70, 78, 82) sts.

Work in Double Moss pat until front measures 13 (13½, 14, 14, 14½, 15, 15) inches from cast-on edge, ending by working a WS row.

Sleeve shaping

Cast on 4 sts at the beg of the next 4 RS rows. (66, 70, 76, 82, 86, 94, 98 sts)

Work even until piece measures 16½ (17½, 18½, 19, 20, 21, 21½) inches from cast-on edge, ending by working a RS row.

Shape neck

Bind off 8 sts at beg of next row.

[Bind off 3 sts at neck edge] twice, slipping first stitch to make smooth sloped neckline.

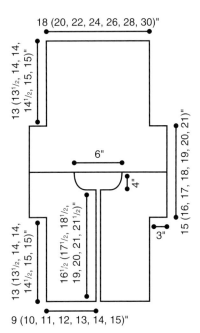

18 (20, 22, 24, 26, 28, 30)"

13 (13½, 14, 14, 15, 15)"

6"

4"

15 (16, 17, 18, 19, 20, 21)"

3"

16½ (17½, 18½, 19, 20, 21, 21½)"

13 (13½, 14, 14, 15, 15)"

9 (10, 11, 12, 13, 14, 15)"

Bind off 2 sts at neck edge, slipping first st. (50, 54, 64, 66, 70, 78, 82 sts)

Work even until front measures 20½ (21½, 21½, 23, 24, 25, 25½) inches from cast-on edge. Sleeve should measure approximately 7½ (8, 8½, 9, 9½, 10, 10½) inches from first underarm cast-on sts.

Place sts on holder.

Right Front

Cast on 50 (54, 60, 66, 70, 78, 82) sts.

Work in Double Moss pat until front measures 13 (13½, 14, 14, 14½, 15, 15) inches from cast-on edge, ending by working a RS row.

Sleeve shaping

Cast on 4 sts at the beg of the next 4 WS rows. (66, 70, 76, 82, 86, 94, 98 sts)

Work even until piece measures 16½ (17½, 18½, 19, 20, 21, 21½) inches from cast-on edge, ending by working a WS row.

Shape neck

Bind off 8 sts at beg of next row.

Bind off 3 sts [at neck edge] twice, slipping first st to make smooth sloped neckline.

Bind off 2 sts [at neck edge] once, slipping first st. (50, 54, 64, 66, 70, 78, 82 sts)

Work even until front measures 20½ (21½, 21½, 23, 24, 25, 25½) inches from cast-on edge. Sleeve should measure approximately 7½ (8, 8½, 9, 9½, 10, 10½) inches from first underarm cast-on sts, ending on same row of Double Moss pat as left front.

Place sts on holder.

Shoulder joining

With RS facing, work across left-front sts, cast on 34 sts for back neck edge, then work right-front sts.

Back

Work in Double Moss pat as established across all sts until back measures 6¾ (7¼, 7¾, 8¼, 8¼, 8¾, 9¼) inches from back neck edge cast-on.

Bind off 4 sts at beg of the next 8 rows. (102, 110, 122, 134, 142, 158, 166 sts)

Work even until back measures same as front from underarm to lower edge.

Bind off all sts.

Neck edging

Hold with RS of right-front neck edge facing, pick up and knit 8 sts across bound-off sts of right front, pick up and knit 30 sts along right-side neck edge; 32 sts across back neck cast-on sts, 30 sts along left-side neck edge and 8 sts across left-front bound-off sts.

Bind off all sts.

Assembly

Sew side and underarm seams.

Flower

Cast on 10 sts.

Row 1: K9 sts, turn.

Row 2: Sl first st, knit to end of row.

Row 3: K8 sts, turn.

Row 4: Sl first st, knit to end of row.

Row 5: K7 sts, turn.

Row 6: Sl first st, knit to end of row.

Row 7: K6 sts, turn.

Row 8: Sl first st, knit to end of row.

Row 9: K5 sts, turn.

Row 10: Sl first st, knit to end of row.

Rows 11 and 12: Rep Rows 7 and 8.

Rows 13 and 14: Rep Rows 5 and 6.

Rows 15 and 16: Rep Rows 3 and 4.

Rows 17 and 18: Rep Rows 1 and 2.

Row 19: Bind off 5 sts, knit across, turn.

Row 20: K5, turn, cast on 5 sts on tip of LH needle.

[Rep Rows 1–20] 4 times to complete a 5-petal flower, on last rep do not cast on 5 sts. Bind off.

Sew final bind off to first 5 sts of cast-on edge.

Follow flower instructions on page 29 to form flower. Weave yarn through center edge sts and gather tightly to close hole. Add beads to center as desired.

Finishing

For button loop, make a slip knot on the crochet hook. Bring the yarn over the hook from back to front and draw through the loop on the hook. Continue to bring the yarn over the hook from back to front and draw through the loop on the hook until there are 20 loops. Fasten off. Fold loop length in half and sew ends to back of flower. Referring to photo for placement, sew flower to left front of sweater. Sew button to WS of right front, opposite loop. Use loop to fasten sweater closed. ■

Short-Sleeve Corsage Cardigan for Girls

Skill Level

EASY

Sizes

Girl's 4 (6, 8/10, 12/14) Instructions are given for smallest size, with larger sizes in parentheses. When only 1 number is given, it applies to all sizes.

Finished Measurement

Chest: 26 (28, 30, 32) inches

Materials

- Lion Brand Microspun lightweight yarn (2.5 oz/168 yds/70g per skein): 3 (3, 3, 4) skeins lime #194
- Size 5 (3.75mm) 29-inch circular needle or size needed to obtain gauge
- Size E/4 (3.5mm) crochet hook (for button loop)
- Stitch holders
- ¾-inch flat button
- Assorted E beads (for flower trim)
- Sewing needle and matching thread

Gauge

22 sts = 4 inches/10cm in Double Moss pat
To save time, take time to check gauge.

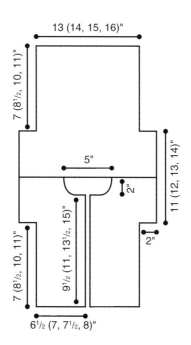

13 (14, 15, 16)"

7 (8½, 10, 11)"

5"

2"

11 (12, 13, 14)"

9½ (11, 13½, 15)"

2"

7 (8½, 10, 11)"

6½ (7, 7½, 8)"

Pattern Stitch

Double Moss (multiple of 4 sts + 2)
Row 1: K1, *k2, p2; rep from * to last st, k1.
Row 2: P1, *k2, p2; rep from * to last st, p1.
Row 3: K1, *p2, k2; rep from * to last st, k1.
Row 4: P1, *p2, k2; rep from * to last st, p1.
Rep Rows 1–4 for pat.

Pattern Notes

Sweater is worked from lower front to lower back with sts cast on at outer edges for sleeves.
Side and underarm seams are sewn after piece is completed.

Left Front

Cast on 34 (38, 42, 46) sts.

Work in Double Moss pat until front measures 7 (8½, 10, 11) inches from cast-on edge, ending by working a WS row.

Shape sleeve

Cast on 4 sts at beg of the next 3 RS rows. (46, 50, 54, 58 sts)

Work even until piece measures 9½ (11, 13½, 15) inches from cast-on edge, ending by working a RS row.

Shape neck

Bind off 8 sts at beg of next row.

Bind off 3 sts [at neck edge] twice, slipping first st to make smooth sloped neckline. (32, 36, 40, 44 sts)

Work even until front measures 11½ (13, 15½, 17) inches from cast-on edge, ending by working a WS row. Sleeve should measure approximately 5½ (6, 6½, 7) inches from first underarm cast-on sts.

Place sts on holder.

Right Front

Cast on 34 (38, 42, 46) sts.

Work in Double Moss pat until front measures 7 (8½, 10, 11) inches from cast-on edge, ending by working a RS row.

Shape sleeve

Cast on 4 sts at beg of the next 3 WS rows. (46, 50, 54, 58 sts)

Work even until piece measures 9½ (11, 13½, 15) inches from cast-on edge, ending by working a WS row.

Shape neck

Bind off 8 sts at beg of next row.

Bind off 3 sts [at neck edge] twice, slipping first st to make smooth sloped neckline. (32, 36, 40, 44 sts)

Work even until front measures 11½ (13, 15½, 17) inches from cast-on edge, ending by working a WS row. Sleeve should measure approximately 5½ (6, 6½, 7) inches from first underarm cast-on sts, ending on same row of Double Moss pat as left front.

Place sts on holder.

Shoulder joining

With RS facing, work across left-front sts, cast on 30 sts for back neck edge, then work across right-front sts.

Back

Work in Double Moss pat as established across all sts until back measures 4¾ (5¼, 5¾, 6¼) inches from back neck edge cast-on.

Bind off 4 sts at beg of the next 6 rows. (70, 78, 86, 94 sts)

Work even until back measures same as front from underarm to lower edge.

Bind off all sts.

Neck edging

Hold with RS of right-front facing, pick up and knit 8 sts across bound-off sts of right front; pick up and knit 22 sts along right-side neck edge, 29 sts across back neck cast-on sts, 22 sts along left-side neck edge and 8 sts across left-front bound-off sts.

Bind off all sts.

Assembly

Sew side and underarm seams.

Flower

Cast on 10 sts.

Row 1: K9 sts, turn.

Row 2: Sl first st, knit to end of row.

Row 3: K8 sts, turn.

Row 4: Sl first st, knit to end of row.

Row 5: K7 sts, turn.

Row 6: Sl first st, knit to end of row.

Row 7: K6 sts, turn.

Row 8: Sl first st, knit to end of row.

Row 9: K5 sts, turn.

Row 10: Sl first st, knit to end of row.

Rows 11 and 12: Rep Rows 7 and 8.

Rows 13 and 14: Rep Rows 5 and 6.

Rows 15 and 16: Rep Rows 3 and 4.

Rows 17 and 18: Rep Rows 1 and 2.

Row 19: Bind off 5 sts, knit across, turn.

Row 20: K5, turn, cast on 5 sts on tip of LH needle.

[Rep Rows 1–20] 4 times to complete a 5-petal flower, on last rep do not cast on 5 sts. Bind off.

Sew final bind off to first 5 sts of cast-on edge.

Follow flower instructions on page 29 to form flower. Weave yarn through center edge sts and gather tightly to close hole. Add beads to center as desired.

Finishing

For button loop, make a slip knot on the crochet hook. Bring the yarn over the hook from back to front and draw through the loop on the hook. Continue to bring the yarn over the hook from back to front and draw through the loop on the hook until there are 20 loops. Fasten off. Fold loop length in half and sew ends to back of flower. Referring to photo for placement, sew flower to left front of sweater. Sew button to WS of right front opposite loop. Use loop to fasten sweater closed. ■

Skill Level

EASY

Sizes

Baby's/toddler's 6 months (1 year, 2 years) Instructions are given for smallest size, with larger sizes in parentheses. When only 1 number is given it applies to all sizes.

Finished Measurement

Chest: 20 (22, 24) inches

Materials

- Lion Brand Microspun lightweight yarn (2.5 oz/168 yds/70g per skein): 2 (2, 3) skeins fuchsia #146, small amount lime #194 (for flower trim)
- Size 4 (3.5mm) 29-inch circular needle or size needed to obtain gauge
- Size E/4 (3.5mm) crochet hook (for button loop)
- Stitch holders
- ¾-inch flat button
- Sewing needle and matching thread

Gauge

22 sts = 4 inches/10cm in Double Moss pat
To save time, take time to check gauge.

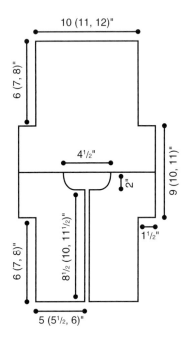

Pattern Stitch

Double Moss (multiple of 4 sts + 2)
Row 1 (RS): K1, *k2, p2; rep from * to last st, k1.
Row 2: P1, *k2, p2; rep from * to last st, p1.
Row 3: K1, *p2, k2; rep from * to last st, k1.
Row 4: P1, *p2, k2; rep from * to last st, p1.
Rep Rows 1–4 for pat.

Pattern Notes

Sweater is worked from lower front to lower back with sts cast on at outer edges for the sleeves.
Side and underarm seams are sewn after piece is completed.

Left Front

Cast on 26 (30, 34) sts.

Work in Double Moss pat until front measures 6 (7, 8) inches from cast-on edge, ending by working a WS row.

Shape sleeve

Cast on 4 sts at beg of next 2 RS rows. (34, 38, 42 sts)

Work even until piece measures 8½ (10, 11½) inches from cast-on edge, ending by working a RS row.

Shape neck

Bind off 6 sts at beg of next row.

Bind off 3 sts [at neck edge] twice, slipping first st to make smooth sloped neckline. (22, 26, 30 sts)

Work even until front measures 10½ (12, 13½) inches from cast-on edge, ending by working a WS row. Sleeve should measure approximately 4½ (5, 5½) inches from first underarm cast on.

Place sts on holder.

Right Front

Cast on 26 (30, 34) sts.

Work in Double Moss pat until front measures 6 (7, 8) inches from cast-on edge, ending by working a RS row.

Shape sleeve

Cast on 4 sts at beg of next 2 WS rows. (34, 38, 42 sts)

Work even until piece measures 8½ (10, 11½) inches from cast-on edge, ending by working a WS row.

Shape neck

Bind off 6 sts at beg of next row.

Bind off 3 sts [at neck edge] twice, slipping first st to make smooth sloped neckline. (22, 26, 30 sts)

Work even until front measures 10½ (12, 13½) inches from cast-on edge, ending by working a WS row. Sleeve should measure 4½ (5, 5½) inches from first underarm cast on sts, ending on same row of Double Moss pat as left front.

Place sts on holder.

Shoulder joining

Work across left front sts, cast on 26 sts for back neck edge, then work across right front sts.

Back

Work in Double Moss pat as established across all sts until back measures 3¾ (4¼, 4¾) inches from back neck edge cast-on.

Bind off 4 sts at beg of the next 4 rows. (54, 62, 70 sts)

Work even until back measures same as front from underarm to lower edge.

Bind off all sts.

Neck edging

Hold with RS of right-front neck edge facing, pick up and knit 6 sts across bound-off sts, pick up and knit 15 sts along right-side neck edge, 24 sts across back neck cast-on sts, 15 sts along left-side neck edge, and 6 sts across left-front bound-off sts.

Bind off all sts.

Assembly

Sew side and underarm seams.

Flower

Cast on 10 sts.

Row 1: K9 sts, turn.

Row 2: Sl first st, knit to end of row.

Row 3: K8 sts, turn.

Row 4: Sl first st, knit to end of row.

Row 5: K7 sts, turn.

Row 6: Sl first st, knit to end of row.

Row 7: K6 sts, turn.

Row 8: Sl first st, knit to end of row.

Row 9: K5 sts, turn.

Row 10: Sl first st, knit to end of row.

Rows 11 and 12: Rep Rows 7 and 8.

Rows 13 and 14: Rep Rows 5 and 6.

Rows 15 and 16: Rep Rows 3 and 4.

Rows 17 and 18: Rep Rows 1 and 2.

Row 19: Bind off 5 sts, knit across, turn.

Row 20: K5, turn, cast on 5 sts on tip of LH needle.

[Rep Rows 1–20] 4 times to complete a 5-petal flower, on last rep do not cast on 5 sts. Bind off.

Sew final bind off to first 5 sts of cast-on edge.

Follow flower instructions on page 29 to form flower. Weave yarn through center edge sts and gather tightly to close hole. With lime, add embroidery to center as desired.

Finishing

For button loop, make a slip knot on the crochet hook. Bring the yarn over the hook from back to front and draw through the loop on the hook. Continue to bring the yarn over the hook from back to front and draw through the loop on the hook until there are 18 loops. Fasten off. Fold loop length in half and sew ends to back of flower. Referring to photo for placement, sew flower to left front of sweater. Sew button to WS of right front opposite loop. Use loop to fasten sweater closed. ■

Flower Instructions

Finished flower should look like photo 1.

Photo 1

To add 3-D shape to flower, poke needle through center, placing right corner of each petal, 1 at a time, on needle (photos 2 and 3).

Photo 2

Photo 3

When all 5 petals are on the needle, the flower will look like a pinwheel (photo 4).

Photo 4

Take each petal, 1 at a time, and fold open (photo 5).

Photo 5

Tack petal open with a stitch or 2 about ¼ to ½ inch from center (photo 6).

Photo 6

Abbreviations & Symbols

approx ....approximately
beg... begin/beginning
CC .... contrasting color
ch.. chain stitch
cm ....centimeter(s)
cn ....cable needle
dec .... decrease/decreases/decreasing
dpn(s) .... double-pointed needle(s)
g ....gram
inc ....increase/increases/increasing
k..knit
k2tog.. knit 2 stitches together
LH...left hand
lp(s)...loop(s)
m.. meter(s)
M1 .... make one stitch
MC .... main color
mm ....millimeter(s)
oz..ounce(s)
p .... purl
pat(s)... pattern(s)
p2tog ....purl 2 stitches together
psso ....pass slipped stitch over
p2sso .... pass 2 slipped stitches over
rem .... remain/remaining
rep...repeat(s)
rev St st ....reverse stockinette stitch
RH ....right hand

rnd(s) ....rounds
RS ....right side
skp ....slip, knit, pass stitch over—one stitch decreased
sk2p .... slip 1, knit 2 together, pass slip stitch
..............over, then knit 2 together—2 stitches have been decreased
sl...slip
sl 1k.. slip 1 knitwise
sl 1p..slip 1 purlwise
sl st.. slip stitch(es)
ssk.....................slip, slip, knit these 2 stitches together—a decrease
st(s) .... stitch(es)
St st.............................. stockinette stitch/stocking stitch
tbl ....through back loop(s)
tog... together
WS .... wrong side
wyib .... with yarn in back
wyif ....with yarn in front
yd(s)...yard(s)
yfwd.. yarn forward
yo .... yarn over

[ ] work instructions within brackets as many times as directed

( ) work instructions within parentheses in the place directed

** repeat instructions following the asterisks as directed

* repeat instructions following the single asterisk as directed

" inch(es)

How to Check Gauge

A correct stitch gauge is very important. Please take the time to work a stitch gauge swatch about 4 x 4 inches. Measure the swatch. If the number of stitches and rows are fewer than indicated under "Gauge" in the pattern, your needles are too large. Try another swatch with smaller-size needles. If the number of stitches and rows are more than indicated under "Gauge" in the pattern, your needles are too small. Try another swatch with larger-size needles.

Skill Levels

BEGINNER
Beginner projects for first-time knitters using basic stitches. Minimal shaping.

EASY
Easy projects using basic stitches, repetitive stitch patterns, simple color changes and simple shaping and finishing.

INTERMEDIATE
Intermediate projects with a variety of stitches, mid-level shaping and finishing.

EXPERIENCED
Experienced projects using advanced techniques and stitches, detailed shaping and refined finishing.

Standard Yarn Weight System

Categories of yarn, gauge ranges, and recommended needle sizes

Yarn Weight Symbol & Category Names	1 SUPER FINE	2 FINE	3 LIGHT	4 MEDIUM	5 BULKY	6 SUPER BULKY
Type of Yarns in Category	Sock, Fingering, Baby	Sport, Baby	DK, Light Worsted	Worsted, Afghan, Aran	Chunky, Craft, Rug	Bulky, Roving
Knit Gauge Range* in Stockinette Stitch to 4 inches	27–32 sts	23–26 sts	21–24 sts	16–20 sts	12–15 sts	6–11 sts
Recommended Needle in Metric Size Range	2.25–3.25mm	3.25–3.75mm	3.75–4.5mm	4.5–5.5mm	5.5–8mm	8mm and larger
Recommended Needle U.S. Size Range	1 to 3	3 to 5	5 to 7	7 to 9	9 to 11	11 and larger

* GUIDELINES ONLY: The above reflect the most commonly used gauges and needle sizes for specific yarn categories.

3-Needle Bind Off

Use this technique for seaming two edges together, such as when joining a shoulder seam. Hold the edge stitches on two separate needles with right sides together.

With a third needle, knit together a stitch from the front needle with one from the back.

Repeat, knitting a stitch from the front needle with one from the back needle once more.

Slip the first stitch over the second.

Repeat, knitting a front and back pair of stitches together, then bind one off.

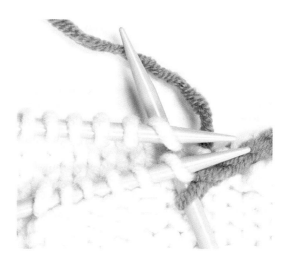

Metric Charts

INCHES INTO MILLIMETERS & CENTIMETERS (Rounded off slightly)

inches	mm	cm	inches	cm	inches	cm	inches	cm
1/8	3	0.3	5	12.5	21	53.5	38	96.5
1/4	6	0.6	5 1/2	14	22	56	39	99
3/8	10	1	6	15	23	58.5	40	101.5
1/2	13	1.3	7	18	24	61	41	104
5/8	15	1.5	8	20.5	25	63.5	42	106.5
3/4	20	2	9	23	26	66	43	109
7/8	22	2.2	10	25.5	27	68.5	44	112
1	25	2.5	11	28	28	71	45	114.5
1 1/4	32	3.2	12	30.5	29	73.5	46	117
1 1/2	38	3.8	13	33	30	76	47	119.5
1 3/4	45	4.5	14	35.5	31	79	48	122
2	50	5	15	38	32	81.5	49	124.5
2 1/2	65	6.5	16	40.5	33	84	50	127
3	75	7.5	17	43	34	86.5		
3 1/2	90	9	18	46	35	89		
4	100	10	19	48.5	36	91.5		
4 1/2	115	11.5	20	51	37	94		

KNITTING NEEDLE CONVERSION CHART

U.S.	1	2	3	4	5	6	7	8	9	10	10 1/2	11	13	15	17	19	35	50
Continental-mm	2.25	2.75	3.25	3.5	3.75	4	4.5	5	5.5	6	6.5	8	9	10	12.75	15	19	25

American School of Needlework ®
excellence in instruction

DRG Publishing
306 East Parr Road
Berne, IN 46711
©2006 American School of Needlework

TOLL-FREE ORDER LINE or to request a free catalog (800) 582-6643
Customer Service (800) 282-6643, **Fax** (800) 882-6643

Visit AnniesAttic.com.

We have made every effort to ensure the accuracy and completeness of these instructions.
We cannot, however, be responsible for human error, typographical mistakes or variations in individual work.

ISBN-10: 1-59012-191-0   All rights reserved.   Printed in USA   1 2 3 4 5 6 7 8 9
ISBN-13: 978-1-59012-191-7